Great Blue Heron

88 Haiku
Inspired By Nature

By
Mary Love

Wild Poet Dreaming

CANADA

Haiku

The haiku poems in this book use the most common haiku structure of three lines containing:

5 syllables

7 syllables

5 syllables

Inspired by natural imagery and using unrhymed lines, these haiku poems are meant to spark your imagination and ignite your senses. Consumed in small bites, haiku can be deeply satisfying, creating imagery that will linger in your mind long after you read them. Such is the joy of haiku.

~ 1 ~

The Great Blue Heron
Standing in quiet patience
I bow to your reign

~ 2 ~

Leaves dance in the wind
Branches hold tight to their stem
Autumn wind cuts in.

~ 3 ~

Moonlight on the snow
Casts a spotlight on the night
We walk centre stage

~ 4 ~

Privilege of flight
Granted to creatures with wings
And all those who dream

~ 5 ~

Lilac trees still grow
In the ruins of old farms
Groundhog digs his holes

~ 6 ~

Dark clouds chase the horse
Hooves thunder over dry ground
Pulling the rain down

~ 7 ~

The tree stands alone
Bending to the whims of wind
A ballet in wood

~ 8 ~

Walking in winter
Trudging through deep snow
I'm melting like summer

~ 9 ~

Old stump sits rotting
Hard wood now crumbles to dust
Sapling sprouts new life

~ 10 ~

Four deer in the yard
Eating apples from the tree
No fear among them

~ 11 ~

Boots stuck in the mud,
Snow giving way to the sun
Buds burst from the trees

~ 12 ~

Tiny little ants
Industrious achievements
Put us all to shame

~ 13 ~

Islands in the lake
Broken land shattered like glass
Stone steps for giants

~ 14 ~

Little green minnows
Darting about with such speed
Hungry bird watches

~ 15 ~

Grey wolf on the shore
Sipping water from the lake
She moves like a ghost

~ 16 ~

Dandelions bloom
Yellow nectar for the bees
Bane of urban man

~ 17 ~

Pretty little creek
Bubbling like happy laughter
You help me to sleep

~ 18 ~

Hiking a worn trail
Joining the steps of others
I forget myself

~ 19 ~

Sleeping on the earth
Open air and stars above
Where we all first slept

~ 20 ~

Sheltered by pine trees
Steady cool rain is falling
A beautiful world

~ 21 ~

Our little blue earth
Sailing the ocean of space
We are stowaways

~ 22 ~

Spider web hanging
Catching me across my face
Like a ghostly veil

~ 23 ~

Romantic dreamers
Who love poetry and art
Know the moon by name

~ 24 ~

My hand touching rock
Millions of years in my palm
The sun is so hot

~ 25 ~

Snow still on the ground
Birds nestled up in the trees
Beckoning the spring

~ 26 ~

Canada goose honks
Calling to her friend the wind
We all know the sound

~ 27 ~

Bare feet to the earth
Head tilted toward the sun
A raven mocks me

~ 28 ~

Thunderstorm erupts
Theatre of light and rain
The moon stays backstage

~ 29 ~

Baby birds in nest
Worms flown to their hungry tongues
So they too can fly

~ 30 ~

Evening darkens
No more shadow beside me
I must walk alone

~ 31 ~

Sunrise calls my name
Pulling me from my soft bed
I hear the birds sing

~ 32 ~

Life will thrive or die
When fierce lightning strikes the earth
I breathe sweet, fresh air

~ 33 ~

Billions of bright stars
Kiss the night through a black veil
Lanterns in the sky

~ 34 ~

Coloured leaves in fall
Each one painted by Nature
My mentor in art

~ 35 ~

Pink salamander
Living beneath old logs
Guarding the fairies

~ 36 ~

Blossoms in the spring
Beautifully scented air
Time to start planting

~ 37 ~

A cool soft rain falls
Gently on the thirsty ground
My soul is refreshed

~ 38 ~

Snow in the highlands
Melts into rising rivers
I toss in my wish

~ 39 ~

Chipmunk digs his holes
Right where I wish he would not
But he always wins

~ 40 ~

Huge orange pumpkins
Carved into grotesque faces
Black bear smells dinner

~ 41 ~

Fishing in the sun
Cast a line in the water
Dragonfly watching

~ 42 ~

Wild turkey feathers
Shimmering touch of colour
Fit for a wild hat

~ 43 ~

Picnic by the lake
Under the shade of tall pines
We devour the view

~ 44 ~

Spring ice, thick or thin?
A walk of Russian roulette
I don't want to lose

~ 45 ~

Trees without their leaves
Grey among the evergreens
Landscape of contrast

~ 46 ~

If I chose to bend
As a tree bends in the wind
Life would be simpler

~ 47 ~

White clouds in the sky
Float in an ocean of blue
Ducks swim with their wings

~ 48 ~

Sweet tiny Screech Owl
Frightened of the Great Horned Owl
Knows how the mouse feels

~ 49 ~

Ruffed Grouse beats her chest
The moment I'm walking by
Pleased she has scared me

~ 50 ~

The crow learned to speak
Slyly listening to me
Without me knowing

~ 51 ~

Spring flowers blossom
Lemon yellow and moss green
The bees are artists

~ 52 ~

My home in the north
Native land of silver birch
Paddle in my hand

~ 53 ~

Rocks under water
Covered in slippery slime
Try to stand up - Splash!

~ 54 ~

Cabin in the woods,
Nestled among the tall trees
The writer soon writes

~ 55 ~

Alone in the dark
Isolated and afraid
A new courage comes

~ 56 ~

Time spent in nature
Reaches deep into our soul
A gentle healing

~ 57 ~

Angled stumps remain
Evidence of the beaver
Goodbye maple trees

~ 58 ~

Swimming in the lake,
Eyes open underwater
I become a fish

~ 59 ~

Bald eagle flying
Shadow dancing on the ground
Partners joined by sun

~ 60 ~

Pussy willows bloom
Cattails swaying in the wind
Red-winged blackbird sings

~ 61 ~

Roar of ocean waves
A storm pounds against the shore
No fishing today

~ 62 ~

Sitting on a rock
Enjoying the midday sun
A turtle joins me

~ 63 ~

Robin pulls a worm
An elastic tug-of-war
Owl has gone to sleep

~ 64 ~

Spider on a boat
Soon regrets the web she weaves
Can't last the voyage

~ 65 ~

Floating on the lake
Canoe drifting in silence
No need to paddle

~ 66 ~

Heron does not move
His eyes following the fish
Beak strikes like lightning

~ 67 ~

Carpet of green moss
Guides me into the forest
I am enchanted

~ 68 ~

Fog on the river
The beaver looks like a log
Drifting with our dreams

~ 69 ~

Weeping willow mourns
As the frosts of fall begin
Her leaves fall like tears

~ 70 ~

Geese on the water
Bossy honking aimed at us
Bullfrog says nothing

~ 71 ~

A waterfall roars
The sound helps to clear my mind
No clouds in the sky

~ 72 ~

Giant pine stands tall
Overseeing the landscape
Hawk feeds on a snake

~ 73 ~

Calm water like glass
A pure reflection of shore
Breathe in the magick

~ 74 ~

One last frost in spring
Becomes winter's final breath
A fawn sniffs the air

~ 75 ~

Mighty Great Horned Owl
Calls to his mate in the night
Such a haunting sound

~ 76 ~

Lay in the sunshine
On a beautiful spring day,
Listen to life grow

~ 77 ~

Two dragonflies dance
Entwined together in flight
Right before my eyes

~ 78 ~

I walk by moonlight
Following a trail of light
Path always changing

~ 79 ~

Squirrel chatters on
Scolding everyone in sight
Raven scolds him back

~ 80 ~

Ripples in a pond
Gliding across the surface
Gentle rings of thought

~ 81 ~

Shells up on the beach
I examine every one
Happy as a child

~ 82 ~

Winter tries to hide
Everything under the snow
Succeeds for a while

~ 83 ~

A murder of crows
Has gathered up in the trees
With big news to tell

~ 84 ~

Walking home at night
Spring peepers call from the pond
Their volume on full

~ 85 ~

Giant moose walking
Long legs look like trees moving
Rabbit darts below

~ 86 ~

Wildflowers growing
Colour and fragrance divine
Hummingbird's delight

~ 87 ~

Snake moves in the grass
Such a terrifying sight
Yet she means no harm

~ 88 ~

Do not try to tame
The wild spirit that is you
Embrace your wildness

www.ingramcontent.com/pod-product-compliance
Lightning Source LLC
Chambersburg PA
CBHW061450050726
47593CB00004B/1523